# EXPLORING THE WORLD

# HUDSON

## Henry Hudson Searches for a Passage to Asia

## BY ROBIN S. DOAK

Content Adviser: Len Travers, Ph.D., Department of History,
University of Massachusetts, Dartmouth, Massachusetts

Reading Adviser: Dr. Linda D. Labbo, Department of Reading Education,
College of Education, The University of Georgia

COMPASS POINT BOOKS
MINNEAPOLIS, MINNESOTA

Compass Point Books
3109 West 50th Street, #115
Minneapolis, MN 55410

Visit Compass Point Books on the Internet at *www.compasspointbooks.com* or
e-mail your request to *custserv@compasspointbooks.com*

Photographs ©: Hulton/Archive by Getty Images, cover, 1, 31; North Wind Picture Archives,
back cover (background), 10, 12, 13, 14, 17, 18, 20, 23, 26, 28, 35, 38; Bettmann/Corbis, 4,
29, 32; Catherine Karnow/Corbis, 5; Stapleton Collection/Corbis, 7; Wolfgang Kaehler/Corbis,
9, 16; Stock Montage, 11, 24; Galen Rowell/Corbis, 15, 40; Lee Snider/Corbis, 21; Neil
Rabinowitz/Corbis, 25; Corbis, 27; Christie's Images/Corbis, 30; Roger Ressmeyer/Corbis,
34; Kennan Ward/Corbis, 37; Tate Gallery, London/Art Resource, N.Y., 39; Alan Schein
Photography/Corbis, 41.

Editors: E. Russell Primm, Emily J. Dolbear, Melissa McDaniel, and Catherine Neitge
Photo Researcher: Svetlana Zhurkina
Photo Selector: Linda S. Koutris
Designer: The Design Lab
Cartographer: XNR Productions, Inc.

**Library of Congress Cataloging-in-Publication Data**
Doak, Robin S. (Robin Santos), 1963–
   Hudson : Henry Hudson searches for a passage to Asia / by Robin S. Doak.
     p. cm. — (Exploring the world)
 Includes bibliographical references and index.
  ISBN 0-7565-0422-8 (hardcover)
  ISBN 0-7565-1144-5 (softcover)
  1. Hudson, Henry, d. 1611—Juvenile literature. 2. America—Discovery and exploration—
English—Juvenile literature. 3. Explorers—America—Biography—Juvenile literature.
4. Explorers—Great Britain—Biography—Juvenile literature. [1. Hudson, Henry, d. 1611.
2. Explorers. 3. America—Discovery and exploration—English.] I. Title. II. Series.
  E129.H8 D63 2003
  910'.92—dc21                    2002009923

# Table of Contents

NOTE: In this book, words that are defined in the glossary
are in **bold** the first time they appear in the text.

# Henry Hudson and the Passage to Asia

In 1607, Henry Hudson began preparing for the first of his four famous journeys of exploration. Hudson was an excellent sailor and an expert **navigator.** He had been hired by the Muscovy Company in England to find a quick route to Asia. Between 1607 and 1611, Hudson made four **voyages** in search of a passage to the riches that could be found in China and Japan. Hudson's voyages and his successes are well known. Although he never found what he was looking for—a shorter route to Asia from Europe—his trips were important. In the 1600s, they added to Europe's knowledge about the

*Henry Hudson was an experienced navigator who used his skills to seek out a faster route to Asia.*

*The Hudson River*

rest of the world. Hudson mapped and explored the coasts of Greenland, Iceland, and many other islands in the Arctic Ocean. He also explored and mapped Hudson Bay, in what is now Canada.

During Hudson's third journey, he became the first European to map and explore the Hudson River region. He claimed the area for the Netherlands. Before long, Dutch settlements in "New Netherlands" sprang up in what is now Connecticut, Delaware, New Jersey, and New York.

Yet some mysteries still surround the adventurer. Where did Hudson come from? How did he gain his knowledge and experience of sailing and the sea? Little is known of Hudson before his 1607 voyage. He may have been born around 1565, but no one knows for sure. There are no written records of his birth, childhood, or early adult years. Some **historians** think that Hudson may have been the grandson of a London public official. Others think that some members of Hudson's family might have been involved with the Muscovy Company.

When Hudson entered the history books in 1607, he was already an able seaman. He must have had experience as a ship's captain to be hired by the Muscovy Company to find a route to Asia. The company was not making much money. It needed Hudson to be successful if it wanted to stay in business.

In 1497, the Portuguese had established the first sea route from Europe to Asia. They made the trip by sailing around the southern tip of Africa. The Portuguese route

Portuguese explorer Vasco da Gama helped to establish his country's sea route from Europe to Asia.

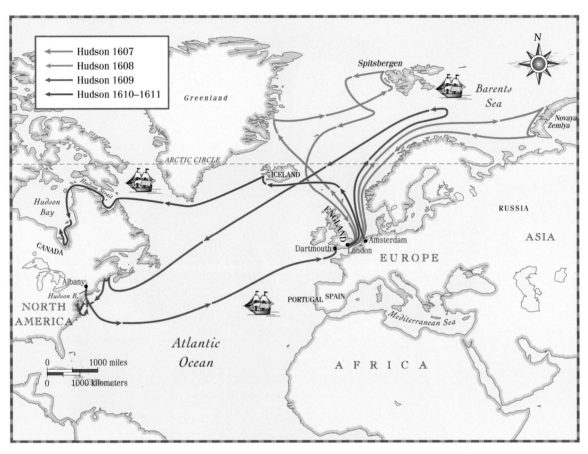

*A map of Hudson's voyages*

was long, difficult, and costly. European explorers had long talked of finding a better route to Asia, where spices and other riches could be found. The rush was on to be the first explorer to find such a route.

# Adventures on the
# *Hopewell*

The English Muscovy Company was eager to be the first to find a northern route to Asia. Since the early 1600s, the Dutch had controlled trade with Asia. As a result, the Muscovy Company had fallen on hard times.

In Hudson's day, some Europeans believed that Asia could be reached by sailing directly across the North Pole. These people reasoned that during the summer, when the pole received twenty-four hours

*Duch galleons like the one shown in this sculpture were used for trade with Asia.*

of sunshine each day, the ice would melt away. First, however, a ship must get beyond the ring of ice around the pole.

In 1607, the Muscovy Company hired Hudson. They gave him command of a ship named the *Hopewell.* It was a small, square-rigged ship with three masts. On April 23, Hudson and his crew of eleven

*Fifteenth century Europeans thought this Arctic ice would melt in summer to create a quicker route to Asia.*

*The* Hopewell *departed London and sailed down the Thames River in 1607.*

set sail from London. Hudson left behind his wife, Katherine, and his sons Oliver and Richard. He brought along his young son John, who would act as his father's cabin boy, or servant.

From London, the *Hopewell* sailed down the Thames River. By the beginning of May, the ship had lost sight of the English coast. For six weeks, Hudson and his crew sailed northwest through the Atlantic. They reached the coast of Greenland on June 15. Hudson and his men continued northward along Greenland's east coast, making their way slowly through thick fog and floating ice.

By the end of June, the *Hopewell* reached Spitsbergen Island, a large island to the east of Greenland. From Spitsbergen, Hudson headed north, hoping to make his way across the North Pole.

*Hudson and his crew saw walrus as they traveled north.*

Along the way, members of his crew spotted many whales, seals, and walrus.

As Hudson made his way north, he began to suspect the worst. By the end of July, he was about 575 miles (925 kilometers) away from the North Pole. No explorer had ever been so close to the pole. Hudson soon realized the *Hopewell* would never make it past the North Pole. Even in midsummer, the Arctic waters were thick with ice. Hudson could see

*The Hopewell faced dangerous icebergs as it drew closer to the North Pole.*

no way to sail through the ice. The *Hopewell* turned around and headed for home.

The *Hopewell* reached London in mid-September. Although Hudson had not succeeded in his goal of finding a route across the North Pole to Asia, the Muscovy Company called his voyage successful. They soon began sending whaling ships to Spitsbergen to hunt whales for their blubber, or fat, and oil. This marked the beginning of the English whaling **industry.**

The following year, the Muscovy Company decided to pay for a second voyage by Hudson. This time, the explorer would sail along the northern coast of Russia in search of a route to Asia. This supposed water route between Europe and Asia was called the **Northeast Passage.**

Once again, Hudson commanded the *Hopewell.*

For this voyage, however, the ship's hull, or body, had been strengthened so it could better make its way through icy waters. Hudson's son John joined him for the second voyage, along with thirteen others. One crew member was Robert

*The icy waters of the Russian Arctic*

*The bad weather along the coast of Norway proved unhealthy for Hudson's crew.*

Juet. He would later play an important role in Hudson's life.

On April 22, 1608, the *Hopewell* sailed out of London's harbor. Hudson sailed northeast, rounding the tip of Norway in late May. The weather was terrible. The cold, fog, and damp made some of the crew very sick.

Ice was a constant danger to the *Hopewell* and its crew. In June, the ship was nearly locked in the ice off the coast of Norway. At other times, the crew kept the ice from their vessel only by pushing it away with oars and poles.

On June 15, two crew members reported seeing something strange in the waters off the ship. Hudson described it as having the body of a woman and the tail of a porpoise. Sailors on later voyages would

*Mermaids are mythical creatures that sailors claim to have seen.*

report seeing similar creatures. These **mythical** figures came to be called mermaids.

In time, the *Hopewell* reached the western coast of two islands to the north of Russia called Novaya Zemlya. There, some of the crew landed and searched for food and water. They returned with deer antlers, whale fins, and reports of seeing bear, deer, and fox tracks.

For more than a week, Hudson searched for a way around or

*The coast of Novaya Zemlya, which means "new land" in Russian*

through the islands. He tried to sail around Novaya Zemlya's northern tip, but ice blocked his way. Then Hudson spotted the mouth of what looked like a big river. He sent some men to check it out. They soon brought back word that the river was too shallow for the ship to travel. Finally, Hudson decided that he would not be able to find a way around Novaya Zemlya. Again, the *Hopewell* headed back to England.

# A Historic Journey Begins

Although Hudson's first two voyages had been unsuccessful, the explorer was still sure that he could find a shorter route to Asia. The Muscovy Company, however, had lost faith in Hudson. It refused to pay for a third journey. The company decided instead to spend its money sending ships to the whaling waters Hudson had discovered in 1607.

Hudson was not ready to give up. He began searching for someone else to pay for his next trip. He turned to the Netherlands and the Dutch East India Company. This company already controlled European trade with Asia, but company officials were still interested in finding a quicker, shorter route to Asia.

The Dutch decided to give Hudson a chance. The explorer had more firsthand knowledge of the Arctic Ocean than anyone else. The company believed Hudson would succeed on his next voyage to find the Northeast Passage.

In January 1609, Hudson signed a **contract** with the Dutch East India Company that

*Hudson appealed to the Dutch East India Company in Amsterdam to finance his next voyage.*

required him to "search for a northeast passage, sailing north around Novaya Zemlya until he shall be able to sail south." The contract also required Hudson to turn over all his journals, **logs,** and charts at the end of the voyage. Just before Hudson set sail, the company added something else: The explorer was not to look for any route but the Northeast Passage.

The Dutch East India Company gave Hudson a small ship called the *Half Moon.*

*A replica of the* Half Moon

This little flat-bottomed ship measured about 60 feet (18 meters) long. It had two high decks on each end. The crew of the *Half Moon* numbered between eighteen and twenty men. Some were Dutch; some were English. Hudson had problems with half of his crew from the start—he did not speak Dutch.

In early April, the *Half Moon* set sail. Hudson steered a course up the coast of Norway. On May 5, the ship rounded Norway's North Cape and began heading east. The crew of the *Half Moon* faced freezing temperatures, icy seas, and thick fog. The ship's sails stiffened and froze in the chilly wind. Its ropes were covered with ice. The Dutch sailors became frightened. They were used to sailing in the warm, tropical waters of southern Asia. As their fear rose, fighting broke out between the Dutch and English sailors.

By mid-May, Hudson's crew was nearing **mutiny,** or rebellion. So Hudson went to his cabin and returned with letters and maps that his friend Captain John Smith had sent him. Smith had explored the coast of North America around Virginia. He had written to Hudson about a large mouth of water there. Perhaps this was the **Northwest Passage,** a **fabled** route through North America to Asia.

*Hudson's crew left Amsterdam in 1609 but was un-prepared for the cold and difficult journey ahead.*

The portraicter of Captayne John Smith / Admirall of New England / The portraictuer of Captayne John Smith

These are the Lines that shew thy Face but those
That shew thy Grace and Glory, brighter bee.
Thy Faire-Discoueries and Fowle-Overthrowes
Of Salvages, much Cwilliz'd by thee
Best shew thy Spirit and to it Glory Wyn;
So, thou art Brasse without—but Golde within.

*Hudson used the maps of John Smith (shown here) to search for the Northwest Passage.*

Using Smith's maps and letters as a guide, Hudson suggested that the *Half Moon* search for the Northwest Passage instead of the Northeast Passage. The crew quickly agreed. Hudson turned the boat around even though his contract with the Dutch East India Company said he could not do so. By May 19, the *Half Moon* was headed for North America.

# Exploring the Hudson River

On July 12, Hudson spotted North America. The ship anchored off the coast of Maine, and Hudson sent his men ashore to cut down trees for a new mast. The old one had been lost during a violent storm.

A group of Native Americans

*The* Half Moon *anchored off the rocky coast of* Maine.

soon paddled out to the *Half Moon* to trade with Hudson's men. One of Hudson's early meetings with North America's native people ended poorly. On July 25, some of the crew went ashore and attacked the natives' campsite. These men drove away the native people and stole their belongings. Hudson set sail early the next morning.

Some of Hudson's crew attacked the Native Americans in Maine.

*Native Americans watched as Hudson and his men entered New York Bay.*

From Maine, Hudson continued down the coast. He sailed as far south as Cape Hatteras in what is now North Carolina. Then Hudson turned the boat around and headed back north. The captain followed the coastline until he reached what is now New Jersey. On September 3, Hudson sailed into what is known today as New York Bay.

Hudson and his crew spent the next few days exploring the region. They met more native people. The natives welcomed the strangers, offering them gifts of corn and tobacco. In his journal, Robert Juet wrote that the native people were "very polite, [although] we dared not trust them." A few days later, some native people attacked Hudson's crew. They wounded three sailors. One man later died.

On September 10, Hudson entered the river that would one day be named for him. The crew was impressed with the river's bounty and beauty. In his log, Juet wrote that "the river

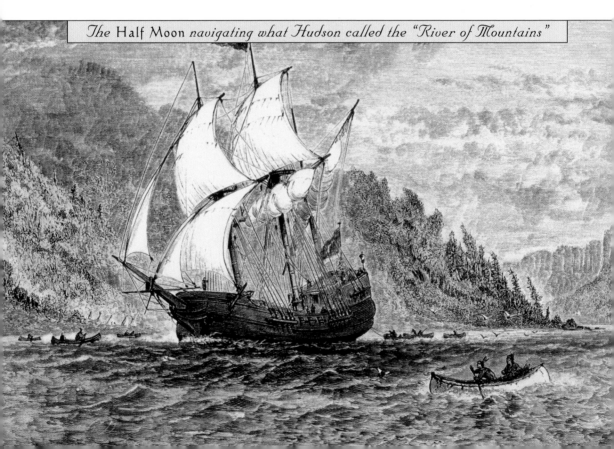

*The* Half Moon *navigating what Hudson called the "River of Mountains"*

is full of fish." Hudson himself called it the "River of Mountains," although the natives of the region called it Muhheakunnuk, or "great waters constantly in motion."

The *Half Moon* sailed about 150 miles (241 km) up the river. Along the way, Hudson and his crew traded with natives they met. The Europeans gave away beads, knives, and hatchets in exchange for beaver skins and otter skins.

*Hudson traded with Native Americans along the river.*

*Hudson realized he wasn't sailing in the Northwest Passage, but he still claimed the area for the Netherlands.*

At a point in the river just north of present-day Albany, New York, Hudson realized that the river was too shallow to be the Northwest Passage. The *Half Moon* began its journey back down the river. Before Hudson left, he claimed the entire region for the Netherlands.

On October 4, the *Half Moon* left North America and began the journey home. On November 7, the ship arrived in Dartmouth, England. No one is sure why Hudson decided to dock in England, especially when he was sailing a Dutch ship for a Dutch company.

Hudson wrote a letter to the Dutch East India Company, telling company officials of his discoveries. They wrote back, ordering Hudson to return to

*When Hudson sailed back to Europe, he docked in England.*

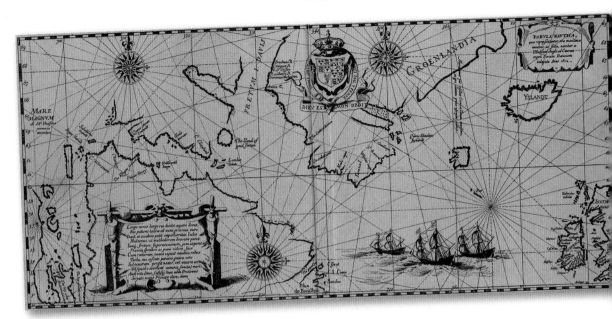

*Hudson's crew took his maps back to the Netherlands.*

the Netherlands at once. By that time, however, Hudson, his ship, and his crew were being held in England.

English officials were furious that Hudson, an Englishman, had been exploring for a rival nation. Hudson was brought to London and placed under **house arrest.** English officials told him that from

then on, he and his English crew must serve only England.

In July 1610, the Dutch crew was finally allowed to sail the *Half Moon* back to the Netherlands. The crew took all of Hudson's logs, maps, and records with them. Unfortunately, these important records of their historic journey later disappeared.

# The Final Voyage

Shortly after Hudson's third voyage, a group of wealthy English merchants began thinking about paying for the explorer's next journey. They hoped that this time, Hudson would be able to find the Northwest Passage.

The ship that would carry Hudson across the Atlantic this time was the *Discovery*. The *Discovery* was an old ship, about 65 feet (20 m) long. Hudson put together a crew of twenty men and two boys. Once again, his son John was on board, listed as the cabin boy. The ship was filled with enough supplies to last eight months.

On April 17, 1610, the *Discovery* left England and sailed northwest toward Iceland. As it passed Iceland, a volcano called Mount Hekla erupted. Some crew members believed this meant their journey would end in disaster. By June 25, the *Discovery* had passed Greenland and entered a long strip of water that connects the Atlantic Ocean to Hudson Bay. Today this body of water is called Hudson Strait.

*Hudson nearly left Juet in Iceland because of his disrespect.*

It took the ship more than a month to travel through the rough and icy waters of Hudson Strait. During that time, the mood among Hudson's men grew worse.

Robert Juet was also causing trouble. Juet did not like or respect Hudson. He was unable or unwilling to keep those feelings to himself. In May, Hudson almost abandoned Juet in Iceland. Hudson later put Juet on trial for mutiny but did not order him off the ship.

*A seventeenth-century map showing Hudson Strait*

On August 4, the *Discovery* entered Hudson Bay. During the next three months, Hudson and his crew explored the big body of water. They measured the depth of the bay in different places and explored the bay's islands and coast.

By the end of October, Hudson realized that he and his crew were stuck in the bay for the winter. The captain sent some of the men ashore to prepare winter shelters. On November 1, the crew hauled the *Discovery* aground and settled in for the winter.

The winter that followed was awful. The freezing temperatures and lack of food caused many of the crew to become sick. In November, one man froze to death. As the harsh winter wore on, the crew found themselves eating frogs and moss to survive. Hudson and his men were the first Europeans to spend the winter in the Arctic.

The crew was trapped in Hudson Bay until June 1611. Only then had enough ice melted for the *Discovery* to begin its journey home. As the ship began to sail, Hudson divided up what was left of the food. Some of the men suspected that Hudson had hidden away extra food for himself and his favorite crew members. They began plotting mutiny. The mutiny was led by Robert Juet and Henry Greene, a former friend of Hudson's.

*Hudson and his crew found it difficult to
survive the harsh climate of Hudson Bay.*

*Juet, Greene, and other rebellious sailors forced Hudson off the* Discovery.

behind his back. Then they forced him and his son John into a small boat. Seven other men, either sick or loyal to Hudson, were also put into the tiny boat.

The men in the small boat had no food and few supplies with them. To set them adrift would mean their certain death. Yet Juet, Greene, and the others did just that. They cut the rope that held the small boat to the ship. Then they sailed the *Discovery* away. This was the last that is known of Hudson.

The following day, Juet, Greene, and other crew members attacked. They seized Hudson and tied his hands

Only six of the men who left

Hudson and some loyal crew members after the mutiny

*Questions remain as to whether Hudson and the other mutiny victims were able to survive after they were set adrift.*

Hudson to die made it back to England. Robert Juet died of starvation. Greene and five others were killed in an attack by Inuit people in July. Finally, in October, the *Discovery* arrived in London. The remaining crew members were never punished for their crime.

What happened to Henry Hudson remains a mystery. Could he have survived in the cold, icy area? Possibly. Perhaps Hudson and his men made their way to shore and were able to set up camp. Perhaps they received help from native people in the area. More probably, however, Hudson and the others died in the small boat.

During his four voyages, Hudson sailed to places that no one had ever before visited. He proved that it was impossible to reach Asia by sailing across the North Pole. He made it possible for the Dutch to begin settling the New York area.

Today, Henry Hudson's name lives on. Hudson Bay and Hudson Strait in Canada, and the Hudson River in New York, are all named for him to honor his voyages of exploration.

*The Hudson River in New York*

# Glossary

**contract**—a legal agreement

**fabled**—mythical legends told in stories

**historians**—people who study past events

**house arrest**—confinement by guards to one's home instead of a prison

**industry**—a business or a trade

**logs**—written records kept by the captain of a ship

**mutiny**—rebellion against a ship's captain

**mythical**—imaginary or not real

**navigator**—the person who sets the course on a ship

**Northeast Passage**—a sought after sea route along the northern coast of Russia between Europe and Asia

**Northwest Passage**—a water route once believed to exist across North America

**voyages**—journeys by sea

# Did You Know?

❧ Some historians believe Henry Hudson began sailing as a teenager. He probably served as a cabin boy and was later promoted to the rank of an apprentice.

❧ Hudson's news that the waters off Spitsbergen Island were filled with whales caused people to call him the "grandfather" of the English whaling industry.

❧ Hudson and his crew referred to the seals and walrus they spotted near Greenland as "sea-horses," or "morses." They became nervous if they spotted a killer whale, which sailors considered bad luck.

❧ Hudson's wife, Katherine, asked the English East India Company to organize a rescue mission after his disappearance. The mission was unsuccessful and didn't even occur until three years after the explorer went missing.

# Important Dates

**c. 1565**

Hudson born
in England

**1608**

Hudson begins his
second voyage on the
Hopewell, *this time
traveling along the
Russian coast in search
of a passage to Asia*

**1610~1611**

Hudson commands the
Discovery *in an attempt to
find the Northwest
Passage; when he reaches
the Arctic Ocean, his crew
mutinies and Hudson is
set adrift, never to be
heard from again*

**1614**

At Katherine Hudson's
request, the English
East India Company
heads an unsuccessful
search to find Hudson

**1609**

The Dutch East India
Company provides Hudson
with the Half Moon *to seek
out the Northeast Passage;
Hudson ends up sailing in
Atlantic waters along the
North American coast and
is able to claim the area
that is present-day New York
for the Netherlands*

**1607**

Hudson explores
Greenland and
the North Pole
as captain of the
Hopewell

44

# Important People

**HENRY GREENE** (?–1611) formerly a friend of Hudson's, he helped lead the mutiny against him and became captain after the explorer was set adrift

**JOHN HUDSON** (?) Henry's son who was a victim of the 1611 mutiny; sailed with his father on several voyages

**ROBERT JUET** (?–1611) member of Hudson's crew who was a leader in the 1611 mutiny

**JOHN SMITH** (1580–1631) friend of Hudson's and an explorer who settled the Jamestown colony in Virginia

# Want to Know More?

## At the Library

Goodman, Joan Elizabeth, and Fernando Rangel. *Beyond the Sea of Ice: The Voyages of Henry Hudson*. New York: Mikaya Press, 1999.

Mattern, Joanne, and Patrick O'Brien. *Henry Hudson*. Austin, Tex: Raintree/Steck-Vaughn, 2000.

Santella, Andrew. *Henry Hudson*. Danbury, Conn.: Franklin Watts, 2001.

## On the Web

For more information on *Henry Hudson,* use FactHound to track down Web sites related to this book.

1. Go to *www.facthound.com*
2. Type in a search word related to this book or this book ID: 0756504228
3. Click on the *Fetch It* button.

Your trusty FactHound will fetch the best Web sites for you!

# Through the Mail

**The New Netherland Project**
New York State Library
Empire State Plaza
CEC 8th Floor
Albany, New York 12230
518/474-6067
For information about the Dutch colony
in what is now New York

# On the Road

**Hudson River Maritime Museum**
One Roundout Landing
Kingston, NY 12401
845/338-0071
To learn more about the history
of the Hudson River

# Index

## About the Author

Robin S. Doak has been writing for children for more than fourteen years. A former editor of *Weekly Reader* and *U*S*Kids* magazine, Ms. Doak has authored fun and educational materials for kids of all ages. Some of her work includes biographies of presidents such as John Tyler and Franklin D. Roosevelt, as well as other titles in this series. Ms. Doak is a past winner of an Educational Press Association of America Distinguished Achievement Award. She lives with her husband and three children in central Connecticut.